Alexanders' Buses 1961 Volume 1

Henry Conn

TOTEM
PUBLISHING

ISBN 978-1-913893-08-8

First published in 2021 by Transport Treasury Publishing Limited. 16 Highworth Close, High Wycombe, HP13 7PJ

Totem Publishing an imprint of Transport Treasury Publishing.

www.ttpublishing.co.uk

Printed in Malta By Gutenberg Press

'Alexanders' Buses 1961 Volume 1' is one of books on specialist transport subjects published in strictly limited numbers and produced under the Totem Publishing imprint using material only available at The Transport Treasury.

Front cover. As from 15 May 1961 Alexanders split into three companies, the Northern Area becoming W Alexander & Sons (Northern) Limited. The first buses to be purchased new by the company would be RB280-RB286, (RRS 590-RRS 597), Alexander bodied Leyland PD3A/3s. This is RB285, (RRS 595) on Rosemount Viaduct on 1 April opposite His Majesty's Theatre, which featured Wedding Fever written by Sam Cree and featuring Jimmy Logan. In 2017, the play would achieve a record-breaking 60 years in production.

Frontis Image. (1) This is Falkirk bus station on 8 July and indicating Bathgate via Avonbridge is AB1, (BMS 110), an Alexander-bodied AEC Regal III new in November 1947. On a number of occasions when our family lived in Whitburn, usually with mum, we would travel to Bathgate and then connect with the Alexanders bus to Falkirk via Westfield, Avonbridge, California, Shieldhill, Glen Village and Falkirk, a journey of around 45 minutes; why, mum liked the Falkirk shops.

Rear cover. This is RB167, (DWG 923), an Alexander-bodied Leyland PD2/12 new in June 1953; RB167 has just completed the 50-minute journey between Alloa and Falkirk bus station via the Kincardine Bridge. Also in view is Scottish Motor Traction B265, (ESC 459), a Duple coach-bodied AEC Regal new in March 1947; B265 would have a little over a year left in service and was noted in late 1962 with the contractor Cruden for staff transport.

Introduction

Rather than write about the history of Alexanders, which has been covered by a number of books, I will cover headlines and stories that made the headlines in the UK from throughout the world that the time period of this book covers.

Three days after the first view in this volume was taken the E-Type Jaguar is launched in the UK. On 8 April the British passenger ship Dara blows up and sinks off Dubai with the loss of 238 crew and passengers. Four days later Yuri Gagarin becomes the first human in space, orbiting the Earth once before returning safely to Earth. Tottenham Hotspur win the Football League for the second time in their history on 17 April and win the FA Cup against Leicester on 6 May becoming at that time only the third in history to complete the double. On the same day as Tottenham win the Football League, the Bay of Pigs invasion of Cuba begins and three days later, Fidel Castro announces the failure of the Bay of Pigs invasion.

On 5 May Alan Shepard becomes the first American in space; fourteen days later Venera 1 becomes the first man-made object to fly by another planet by passing Venus. On 21 May the Alabama governor declares martial law in an attempt to restore civil order after race riots break out. Six days later President John F Kennedy, who was sworn in on 20 January, announces to Congress the Apollo programme to put a man on the moon before the end of the decade.

The article written by Peter Benenson, The Forgotten Prisoners, is published and this article is later considered to be the founding of the human rights organisation Amnesty International.

On 4 June President John F Kennedy and Russian president Nikita Khrushchev meet in Vienna to discuss nuclear disarmament, nuclear tests and Germany. Twelve days later the ballet dancer Rudolf Nureyev requests asylum while in Paris with the Kirov Ballet. The Soviet submarine K19 suffers a radiation leak in the North Atlantic on 4 July and three weeks later John F Kennedy gives a widely-watched TV speech on the Berlin crisis, warning "we will not be driven out of Berlin." Kennedy urges Americans to build fallout shelters, setting off a four-month debate on civil defence. On 7 August Vostok 2 with Gherman Titov on board becomes the second man to orbit the Earth and the first to be in orbit for more than a day. Three days later the UK applies for membership of the European Economic Community. Construction of the Berlin Wall begins on 13 August, restricting movement between East Berlin and West Berlin, and forming a clear boundary between West Germany and East Germany, Western Europe and Eastern Europe. On 22 August Ida Siekmann jumps from a window in her tenement building trying to flee to the West, becoming the first of at least 138 people known to have died at the Wall.

This book is a picture album (not intended to be a history of the company), and features views from the period 1 April through to 13 August 1961. Many of the views were taken after 15 May when Alexanders were split into three new companies; Alexander Fife, Midland and Northern with approximately 500, 950 and 450 vehicles respectively. The only noticeable change is that new buses ordered by the new companies have local registrations, such as the Leyland PD3s delivered to Alexander Northern have Aberdeen registrations. Views featured in this volume are in chronological order starting with Aberdeen, then Edinburgh, Larbert, Falkirk, Kirkcaldy back to Edinburgh, Larbert, back to Falkirk, Bannockburn, Stirling and then Edinburgh including views at Easter Road.
The second 1961 volume will feature views in chronological order taken in Kirkintilloch, Kilsyth, Larbert, Leven, St Andrews, Dundee, Falkirk, Perth, Stirling, Bannockburn, Lochgelly and Cowdenbeath, the last view being taken on 26 November 1961.

All the views in each volume are unpublished. Enjoy the nostalgia, and please forward any comments or thoughts to me, I look forward to reading them via the publisher.

I would like to thank Robin Fell for access to the wonderful collection of Alexander buses and coaches negatives from 1961 this book would not have been possible, my sincere thanks.

Henry Conn, August 2021

2. All the views in Aberdeen were taken on 1 April. Standing in Blackfriars Street after having completed the two and a half hour journey from Macduff is A42, (AWG 629), an Alexander-bodied AEC Regal I new in April 1947; A42 would be one of the last 1947 AEC Regal Is to be withdrawn and was noted with a dealer in Peterhead in September 1964.

3. With Union Terrace in the background, RA61, (CMS 364), an Alexander-bodied Leyland PD1, is in the short section of road between Union Terrace and Rosemount; from new in August 1949, RA61 would have a service life of over 21 years.

CADENHEAD'S
GREEN LABEL
DEMERARA
RUM
2B
RA62
CMS 365

Left. (4) Service 2B was between Bieldside and Waterton Road via Cults, Great Western Road, 21 Union Terrace and Bucksburn. On layover in Union Terrace was this RA62, (CMS 365), an Alexander-bodied Leyland PD1 new in August 1949. The imposing granite buildings behind are Aberdeen Central Library, to the left of the view, which was opened on 5 July 1892 by Andrew Carnegie, and St Mark's Church, also built in 1892.

Above. (5) The statue just visible to the right is of William Wallace which was sculpted by William Grant Stevenson and erected in 1888. Passing the statue is RB130, (DMS 490), an Alexander-bodied Leyland PD2/3 new in October 1951 and exported to the USA in October 1971.

6. I think this view, please correct me if I am wrong, is in Gairn Terrace, near the Alexanders' depot. Alexander took delivery of twenty Alexander-bodied Leyland OPS2/1s in January 1952, the OPS indicating the export range. It is thought that the twenty were for export but the order was cancelled. Alexander had them converted to Leyland PS1s in 1960 by the use of parts from redundant PS1s.

NO MENTION OF EIGHT-FOOT-WIDE BODY!

7. On 1 March 1950 Alexanders acquired the vehicles from J Sutherland of Peterhead. In Mealmarket Street, this is Peterhead-based PA199, (EAV 460), a Duple coach-bodied Leyland PS1, new to Sutherland in March 1948; this lovely coach survived with Alexander Northern until 1969.

8. My thoughts with this view taken at Mealmarket Street are that Burnett's Motors of Mintlaw would be purchased by Alexander Northern on 9 January 1967, hence the relevance of the view. This is (ESA 650), a Burlingham-bodied Albion CX13, one of four purchased new by Burnett in 1948; this bus is destined for a journey to Stuartfield, a short distance from its home base in Mintlaw. All the Albions would be withdrawn before Alexander Northern acquired Burnetts.

9. With the hot-off-the-press Press & Journal or Evening Express papers being loaded on, this is Peterhead-based AC7, (FMS 754), an Alexander-bodied AEC Reliance new in March 1955. The headline for the Evening Express on this Saturday would be the threat of a plot to kidnap President Kennedy's three-year-old daughter Caroline, and on at the Capitol would be the first showing of The Canadians with Robert Ryan.

Above. (10) Standing outside the Central Library on Rosemount, just arrived from Inverness, is Huntly-based AC105, (JWG 685), an Alexander coach-bodied AEC Reliance new in June 1957.

Left. (11) A few passengers are ready for the service between Aberdeen and Rosehearty via Fraserburgh; this is Rosehearty-based AC126, (JWG 706), an Alexander-bodied AEC Reliance new in June 1957. In view is the John Smith-designed North Church which opened in 1831. Closed in 1954 it was used as the Aberdeen Arts Centre.

Right. (12) Turning from Rosemouth Viaduct into Union Terrace is AC164, (NMS 376), an Alexander-bodied AEC Reliance new in March 1960.

ABERDEEN
001
NMS 376

13. We are now in Union Street with, in the distance, the imposing Town House and the Salvation Army Citadel buildings can be seen. Working the very regular service between Dyce and Culter is RB208, (NWG 897), an Alexander lowbridge-bodied Leyland PD3/3 new in January 1960.

14. In Union Terrace with the William Wallace monument as a backdrop, this is RB240, (OMS 314), an Alexander-bodied Leyland PD3/3 new in September 1960.The car in view is a Fife-registered Morris Cowley 1200, which were produced between 1954 and 1956.

15. This is RB240 again; from the 1950s onwards, there were several memorable advertising campaigns by the Milk Marketing Board. Slogans included "full of natural goodness, is your man getting enough?" and "milk's gotta lotta bottle" written by the advertising executive Rod Allen, and "drinka pinta milka day" and "had your daily pinta yet?", designed by the advertising agency Ogilvy.

WHY UNDERLINE?

16. The billboards were always fascinating and this one depicts all the best from Macintosh's, Munchies, Rolo, Caramac and Toffo-o-Luxe. If my memory serves me right I think Toffo-o-Luxe was toffee in roll form and the wrapper was red; individually wrapped toffees took over and this sweet was renamed Toffo. Heading for Dyce is RB244, (OMS 318), an Alexander-bodied Leyland PD3/3 new in September 1960.

17. With driver ready, RB285 is about to take up duties on route 8A between Aberdeen and Inverurie, from Blackfriars Street, via Bucksburn, Blackburn and Kintore.

18. On 15 May a total of 29 Alexander coach-bodied Leyland TS7s new in 1937 transferred to Alexander Northern. Representing this batch is P387, (WG 5526), new in April of that year; P387 would be withdrawn late in 1962 and noted with a Stonehaven contractor in January 1963 as staff transport.

19. Twelve Leyland TS8 Specials were transferred to Alexander Northern on 15 May. Turning into Blackfriars Street is P614, (WG 9007), an Alexander coach-bodied TS8 special new in March 1940; all twelve would be withdrawn and sold by December 1963.

20. At the Gairn Terrace depot of Alexanders in Aberdeen was R331, an all-Leyland TD7 new in December 1941; the bodywork was supplied by Leyland and completed by Alexander. During 1962 R331 was on loan to Alexander Midland, but not used and was sold to a dealer for scrap in September 1962. In contrast, in the background is NL23, (RSC 427), an Alexander coach-bodied Albion MR11L new as an Albion demonstrator in June 1958 and was acquired by Alexander shortly afterwards; the vehicle became a bus for handicapped children in Dundee during 1974.

21. The Alexander bus fleet has now been split into three companies as it is 15 June, a month after the split. This is St Andrew bus station and this is PC55, (EMS 173), an Alexander coach-bodied Leyland PSU1/15 new in July 1953 and allocated to Aberdeen in the Alexander Northern fleet.

Above. (22) This is St Andrew Square in Edinburgh and on tour is W250, (EMS 833), a Burlingham-bodied Bedford SB new in May 1953. All but one of the 1953 Bedfords passed to Alexander Midland; W250 in this view is allocated to Kilsyth depot. The car in the background is a Hillman Minx.

Right. (23) Back to St Andrew Square bus station and working the regular service 323 to Stirling via Turnhouse, Winchburgh, Linlithgow, Falkirk and Larbert is the Bannockburn-allocated PD126, (KMS 495), an Alexander coach-bodied AEC Reliance new in March 1958. At this time, if my memory serves me, the only covered area of the bus station was the lane above where PD126 is.

STIRLING
323
KMS 495

24. At Larbert depot on 1 July is another of the Burlingham-bodied Bedford SBs, this is W249, (EMS 832), and at the time this view was taken W249 was allocated to Pitlochry depot. All of the Alexander Midland Bedford SBs were withdrawn in 1966 and W249 was later noted with a contractor in Aberdeen in March 1968. The Alexander Northern-allocated Bedford SB, W242, became a mobile shop in February 1968.

25. This is Falkirk bus station on 1 July and this is R119, (WG 4473), an Alexander-bodied Leyland TD4 new in November 1936; within three months of this view R119 would be sold.

26. Indicating that it may have worked route 78 between Falkirk and Airdrie, at its home depot of Larbert on 1 July is P579, (WG 8796), an Alexander-bodied Leyland TS8 new in June 1939.

27. In February 1938 Alexanders took over the large fleet of Simpson's & Forrester's of Dunfermline. I have included this view as only six ex-Simpson's & Forrester's vehicles survived to the split of Alexanders in May 1961. This is R406, (AFG 662), originally with a single-deck body by Alexander new in June 1935. The chassis was re-built and it received a new double-deck Alexander body in October 1943; R406 is seen here in a withdrawn condition at the back of Larbert depot on 8 July.

28. Standing in Larbert depot before the journey to Falkirk, this is the brand-new PD222, (RMS 711); note that PD222 is missing the plate for depot allocation. This coach was amongst the first coaches to be acquired new by the new company Alexander Midland.

29. Journeying from Larbert depot to Falkirk this is W254, (HMS 221); ten Burlingham-bodied Bedford SBGs were bought new in May 1956 and all had been withdrawn by late 1967 with MW254 being noted with two operators in the Lennoxtown area in 1968, H McEwan first and then Graham & MacGregor.

Above. (30) Not too far from Falkirk bus station was the layover area for the buses and coaches. An interesting line-up in this view with, nearest the camera, PC16, (CMS 382), an Alexander coach-bodied Leyland PSU1/15 new in May 1952. Next in line is W254, (HMS 221), a Burlingham-bodied Bedford SBG new in May 1956, then PC58, (EMS 513), an Alexander coach-bodied Leyland PSU1/15 new in July 1953; note the slight design differences on the front of PC16 and PC58. Last, but not least, the new generation of Alexander coaches, this is brand new PD222, (RMS 711), an Alexander coach-bodied Leyland PSUC1/2.

Right. (31) Back into Falkirk bus station on 8 July and this is Grangemouth-allocated RB107, (DMS 341), an all-Leyland PD2/12 new in November 1951; RB 107 is working service 83B between Grangemouth and Maddiston via Falkirk bus station, Laurieston, Redding Cross Roads and Brightons Cross with a journey time of around 30 minutes.

There's SUNSHINE in..
OUTSPAN
MADDISTON
83B
RB107
G
DMS 341

32. On 15 July, this is possibly one of the last views of P435, (WG 6425), an Alexander-bodied Leyland TS7 new in December 1937 in service; P435 would be sold in November 1961. Allocated to Kirkcaldy depot, P435 is working Kirkcaldy town service 5 between the High Street and Dysart.

33. We are now in the Alexander Fife depot in Kirkcaldy and out of the twenty Leyland OPS2/1s in the Alexander fleet, half were transferred to the new Alexander Fife company; this is PB3, (DMS 816) surrounded by 4 Guy Ara bs and a Leyland PD2/3.

MENTION 8FT BODY ON 7FT 6IN CHASSIS! !!

34. We are now in St Andrew Square on 16 July and Stirling-allocated PD76, (JMS 194), an Alexander coach-bodied Leyland PSUC1/2, has completed the service between Stirling and Edinburgh and is on layover. Behind PD76 is Scottish Motor Traction AA582, (OWS 582), an ECW-bodied Bristol LD6G new in April 1957; later AA582 would pass to Highland Omnibuses in August 1973 and be withdrawn before the end of that year.

35. At the same time as the previous view, still in St Andrew Square, this is PD192, (OMS 268), an Alexander-bodied Leyland PSUC1/2 new in July 1960; note that PD192 lacks a depot allocation plate.

36. It is now 27 July and this, I think, is an interesting view in Larbert depot. This is a freshly re-painted RB201, (KWG 662), an Alexander-bodied Leyland PD3/3 new in August 1958; one could presume that RB201 was involved in an accident, hence the re-paint in the Alexander livery. The re-paint in Alexander Midland livery began in early 1962 so I suspect the RB201 would be one of the last in line for a re-paint.

37. As noted on the front cover, seven Alexander-bodied Leyland PD3A/3s were the first buses to be ordered by Alexander Northern. Sporting an Aberdeen registration number, this is RB293, (RRS 583) at Larbert depot waiting to be delivered to the new company.

Above. (38) Alexander Midland purchased eighteen Alexander-bodied Leyland PD3A/3s, RB262-RB279, (SWG 618-SWG 635). Also in Larbert depot, brand new and sporting their depot allocation plate, are RB266 and RB262.

Right. (39) The old and the very new; standing withdrawn is R120, (WG 4474), an all-Leyland TD4 new in November 1936, and after this view was taken R120 passed to Sowerby's Tours of Gilsland where it remained until scrapped in March 1966. The new is Alexander Northern RB286, (RRS 597), another of the Alexander-bodied Leyland PD3A/3s yet to be delivered to Alexander Northern.

010
LEYLAND
RRS 597
R120
LEYLAND
WG 4474

40. In service to Linlithgow at Larbert is RA32, (BWG 77), an Alexander-bodied Leyland PD1 new in May 1948. The car with fins is a 1960 Singer Gazelle IIIA, introduced September 1959, which gained small tail fins and a larger windscreen. The engine was upgraded with twin Solex carburettors replacing the single Solex, distinguishing it from the Minx, and lifting output to 60 bhp. Home market cars got a floor gear change and as well as overdrive, Smith's Easidrive automatic transmission also became an option.

41. The last view taken on 27 July, working a local Falkirk service 95 between Lochgreen Road and Dawson Park, is of R284, (WG 9198), a Leyland TD7 new in March 1940. The car is a Standard Vanguard Phase III with a local registration new in 1958.

42. The next day standing in Queen Street is Aberdeen-based PC31, (DWG 527), an all-Leyland coach-bodied PSU1/15 new in May 1952; PC31 would remain with Alexander Northern until February 1972. Exiting from St Andrew Square on North St David Street is a Scottish Motor Traction AEC Regent III.

43. This is PD166, (MWG 381), an Alexander coach-bodied Leyland PSUC1/2 new in May 1959; PD166 has just exited St Andrew bus station in service on the 322 to Crieff, a journey of close to 3 hours.

44. In Queen Street this is PD170, (MWG 385), an Alexander coach-bodied Leyland PSUC1/2 new in May 1959; Bannockburn-allocated PD170 has just completed service 321 between Callander and Edinburgh, a journey of over two-and-a-half hours. Behind PD170 is an Austin A30 'Countryman' estate, which were first produced in 1954.

45. All the views taken on 29 July are in or around Falkirk bus station. During January 1961 Trimdon Motor Services took delivery of six Duple Midland Ford Thames 570Es, (1451 PT-1456 PT). Demonstrating with Alexander Midland is (1451 PT), working the service between Glasgow, Buchanan Street, and Bo'ness which had a journey time of around 40 minutes.

46. With a poorly set up destination display, this is RO469, (AMS 110), a Brush-bodied Daimler CWA6 new in August 1944; RO469 passed to Highland Omnibuses in April 1964 but sadly was never operated.

47. Leaving Falkirk bus station for the 50-minute journey to Stirling is Stirling-based RA36, (BWG 81), an all-Alexander-bodied Leyland PD1. Just behind, arriving from Edinburgh on a 323 to Stirling, is PD112, (KMS 481), an Alexander coach-bodied Leyland PSUC1/2 new in September 1957.

48. Route 76 from Falkirk to Bathgate via Armadale was not a particularly frequent service. A few of the journeys of the 76 went via Woodend Colliery, which at the time this view was taken had a workforce of around 500; the colliery closed in 1965. This is PA89, (BWG 315), an Alexander coach-bodied Leyland PS1 new in July 1948; PA89 was acquired by Highland Omnibuses in June 1967 where it was in service for a short time.

49. A regular service between Falkirk and Dunfermline was route 90 via Carronshore, Kincardine, Culross and Cairneyhill. With a healthy load of passengers, about to journey to Dunfermline is Larbert-allocated PA139, (CMS 208), an Alexander coach-bodied Leyland PS1 new in September 1949.

50. All twenty of the Alexander-bodied AEC Regent IIIs new in 1951 were transferred to Alexander Midland. This is RC14, (CWG 877), indicating route 81C, the Falkirk to Grangemouth Circular, outer circle. Working an 81D, the Falkirk to Grangemouth Circular, inner circle, is A72, (BMS 106), a Burlingham-bodied AEC Regal new in September 1947.

51. Leaving Falkirk on route 7 to Glasgow Buchanan Street via Bonnybridge and Cumbernauld is Stepps-based AC11, (FMS 758), a Park Royal-bodied AEC Reliance new in July 1954. The car heading in the opposite direction is a Glasgow-registered Ford Consul.

52. Route 79 between Falkirk bus station and Airdrie via Slamannan was a regular service with a journey time of around 50 minutes. Passengers are aboard but no sign of the crew; this is Grangemouth-based AC19, (FMS 766), a Park Royal-bodied AEC Reliance new in September 1954.

53. This is AC163, (NMS 374), an Alexander-bodied AEC Reliance new in March 1960; in this view AC163 is in service to Edinburgh, limited stop according to the stickers, but no route number is displayed. At the time of the split this coach was transferred to Alexander Northern and if so the depot code plate is for Peterhead. The car is an Edinburgh-registered Austin A40 Somerset.

54. Leaving Falkirk bus station on an 88A to Stirling via Camelon is RB 212, (NWG 901), an Alexander-bodied Leyland PD3/3 new in January 1960. The ECW-bodied Bristol LD6G RD97, (MMS 749), new in May 1959, is working route 71 between Falkirk bus station and Dunipace, a journey time of around thirty minutes. The Bedford Dormobile behind was first registered in West Lothian.

UNUSUAL POSITION FOR ALLOCATION PLATE

55. With a very full load of passengers, leaving Falkirk for Glasgow via Kilsyth is Kilsyth-allocated RB242, (OMS 316), an Alexander-bodied Leyland PD3/3 new in September 1960.

56. The double tea pot means I am having one of those days? Awaiting the driver for a 321 to Edinburgh from Callander is AC209, (RMS 743), an Alexander bodied AEC Reliance new in May 1961. The journey from Falkirk to Edinburgh will take just over the hour.

57. The Falkirk to Linlithgow route 88 was a short journey of around twenty-five minutes and working this route is elderly R272, (WG 9196), an all-Leyland TD7 new in March 1940 and which would still be in the Alexander Fleet until early 1963.

58. With a very informative display, this is R318, (WG 9547), an all-Leyland TD7 ew in January 1941; the circular is route 70, the Larbert Depot circular. Behind, working route 94 between Gibsongray Street and Windsor Road, is RB160, (DWG 916), an Alexander-bodied Leyland PD2/12 new in June 1953.

59. In the bus park in Falkirk, this is R319, (WG 9548), an all-Leyland TD7 new in January 1941. Next in line is P598, (WG 8991), an Alexander-bodied Leyland TS 8 new in March 1940 with an indicator set for route 98 between Falkirk and Camelon. Last in the line is AC31, (FWG 35), a Park Royal-bodied AEC Monocoach new in January 1955.

60. The last of the views taken on 29 July features R333, (WG 9642), an all-Leyland TD7 new in February 1942. Arriving in Falkirk from Stirling is RC3, (CWG 866), an Alexander-bodied AEC Regent III new in February 1951.

61. Standing withdrawn at Larbert on 12 August is R248, (WG 8267), an all-Leyland TD5 new in May 1949; R248 passed to Alexander Fife in May 1961 and in this view is indicating route 306, the Dunfermline to Leven service via the coast. Note that the depot allocation plate has been removed and R248 would be scrapped a month after this view was taken.

62. On the same day in Falkirk, this is very new RB267, (SWG 623), an Alexander-bodied Leyland PD3A/3 allocated to Larbert depot and working route 75A between Stirling and Falkirk via Airth with a journey time of just under the hour.

63. In Falkirk bus station also working the 75A between Falkirk and Stirling is RB260, (RMS 692), one of the seventeen Leyland PD3/3Cs which were re-built from Leyland PS1 chassis and second-hand Leyland engines with new Alexander frames; RB260 was new in March 1961.

64. From Falkirk bus station on 12 August we have travelled to Bannockburn depot. Indicating route 54, a local Stirling service between Woodside Road and Cambusbarron is P576, (WG 8793), an Alexander-bodied Leyland TS8 new in June 1939; P576 would remain in the Alexander Midland fleet until sale in December 1962.

65. The largest customer in Scotland for the Leyland PSUC1 was Alexanders who took two hundred between 1954 and 1964. The first to be delivered arrived in June 1954; exiting Bannockburn depot this is PD26, (FMS 743), an Alexander coach-bodied Leyland PSUC1/2 new in August 1954.

66. Standing in the corner of Stirling depot is C2, (CMS 3), a Scottish Aviation-bodied Commer Commando which was new in April 1949. Only nine Commer Commandos survived to pass to Alexander Midland in May 1961, the remainder of a large batch were withdrawn by Alexanders between 1952 and early 1961. Scottish Aviation were based in Prestwick, originally a flying school operator the company took on aircraft maintenance work in 1938 and was involved in aircraft fitting and maintenance, particularly for the Liberator bomber, during the war; after the war the company diversified into the manufacture of coach and bus bodywork; C2 would be sold to MacKenzie of Achiltibuie, 10 miles north west of Ullapool in May 1963.

67. We have travelled a short distance to Stirling bus station and this is Alloa-allocated PD85, (JMS 203), an Alexander-bodied AEC Reliance new in October 1956. Route 14C is a 40-minute journey between Stirling bus station and Clackmannan. In the background is PD166, (MWG 381), an Alexander coach-bodied Leyland PSUC1/2 new in May 1959; PD166 is working a 322 from Edinburgh to Crieff, which should take around an hour to reach its destination.

68. The last view taken on 12 August is of AC117, (JWG 697), an Alexander coach-bodied AEC Reliance new in June 1957 at Stirling bus station. Displaying the typical Edinburgh Limited Stop sticker on the window, AC117 was transferred to Alexander Northern in May 1961, yet the legal lettering has not been changed and the route displayed, 11, is between Milngavie and Glasgow, confused, hopefully the passengers are not.

69. In St Andrew Square on 13 August is Stirling-based PC19, (CMS 385), an Alexander-bodied Leyland PSU1/15 new in May 1952: PC19 is indicating route 320 between Edinburgh and Aberdeen. I think, in 1961, there was only a single daily journey each day, each way, and they would meet in Dundee bus station at just after 1:00pm.

70. The Aberdeen-Edinburgh service may have only had one journey each day, but there were on many occasions more than one coach working. In St Andrew Square bus station is coach 5 from Aberdeen; this is Aberdeen-allocated PC33, (DWG 529), an all-Leyland PSU1/15 new in May 1952. Parked to the left of this view are a Burlingham-bodied Bedford SB and an Alexander-bodied AEC Regal both with the Scottish Motor Traction fleet.

71. Just arrived at St Andrew bus station is PD204, (FCS 451), an Alexander coach-bodied Leyland PSUC1/2 new as a demonstrator in April 1954; PD204 passed to Lowland Motorways in May 1955. On 13 January 1958 Lowland Motorways was acquired by SMT and PD204 remained in the SMT fleet until exchanged with an AEC Monocoach with Alexanders in May 1960.

72. A narrow and busy lane in St Andrew Square bus station. Soon to leave for Alloa via Bo'ness and Kincardine is Alloa-based AC141, (KWG 565), an Alexander coach-bodied AEC Reliance new in May 1958. Third in line is SMT AA720, (SWS 720), an ECW-bodied Bristol LD6G new in February 1959, and squeezing in at the far end is a 1958 ECW-bodied Bristol LD6G.

ALLOA
325
BO'NESS
A
KWG 565

73. The Albion Aberdonian was an underfloor-engined bus designed and manufactured by Albion Motors between 1957 and 1960, and was a longer derivative of the Albion Nimbus. The Aberdonian was designed to be the lightest full-size underfloor-engined bus available and bodied examples would weigh half a ton less than the similarly-powered Leyland Tiger Cub. Aberdeen-based NL21, (KWG 596) with Alexander coach bodywork was new in June 1958 and is coach 7 arrived from Aberdeen.

74. When Alexanders split into three in May 1961, Alexander Midland received one Aberdonian, Alexander Fife received five and Alexander Northern had the remaining fourteen. The power unit on launch was a Leyland O350H 97 bhp 5.76 litre four-stroke direct-injection six-cylinder diesel, mounted horizontally in mid-wheelbase driving through a unit-mounted Albion clutch and constant mesh gearbox. Some operators found the Aberdonian underpowered, the vacuum brakes were not as effective as the air brakes of the Leyland Tiger Cub, and the Albion clutch gave problems and was replaced by the Leyland unit fitted to the Tiger Cub. A number of the Aberdonians were still with the Alexander Northern fleet in 1975.

75. Another Alexander coach-bodied Leyland PSUC1/2 new in April 1954 to Lowland Motorways was acquired via SMT in May 1960 in exchange for another AEC Monocoach. This was PD203, (LYS 943), seen here unloading passengers in St Andrew Square as coach 3 from Aberdeen.

Alexander's
EDINBURGH
LYS 943

76. On 19 August 1961 Hibs played Celtic in a Scottish League Cup group stage game; the score was 2-2 and the attendance was over 22,000. The next five views were all taken at Easter Road on that day. New to Lawson in July 1954, this is Kilsyth-allocated PD22, (DSN 491), an Alexander-bodied Leyland PSUC1/2 still in Lawson's livery three months after the split.

77. In May 1957 Alexanders took delivery of five Alexander coach-bodied Albion MR9Ls, N1-N5, (JMS 388-JMS 392). Without an allocation plate and in Lawson livery this is N1, (JMS 388); N1-N4 operated in the Lawson's fleet until the split in May 1961, and all five Albions were withdrawn in 1968.

78. In contrast to the two previous views and the next two, this is a rather newer coach for the travelling supporters; this is PD222, (RMS 711), an Alexander-bodied Leyland PSUC1/2 purchased new by Alexander Midland after the split in July 1961.

79. An interesting view; P542, (WG 8121), with a Kilsyth allocation plate, is an Alexander coach-bodied Leyland TS8 new in May 1939 which was transferred to Alexander Fife in May 1961, and was noted in the well-known scrapyard of Muir of Kirkcaldy in December 1961. As far as I am aware, P542, was working in the Fife area!!

80. Another supporters' bus, this is P682, (WG 9518), an Alexander-bodied Leyland TS8 special new in December 1940. The Leyland TS8 Special had the front bulkhead moved forward, leaving a smaller driver's cab and this arrangement increased seating from 35 to 39. A total of 105 specials were delivered and numerically the last was P682; wartime restrictions brought the flow of specials to a halt.